The Donner Party:
The Will to Survive

The Donner Party:

The Will to Survive

Authors

Benjamin A. Turner

Dr. Austin A. Mardon

Catherine Mardon

Editor

Jessica Jutras

Copyright © 2022 by Austin Mardon

All rights reserved. This book or any portion thereof may not be reproduced or used in any manner whatsoever without the express written permission of the publisher except for the use of brief quotations in a book review or scholarly journal.
First Printing: 2022

Cover Design and typeset by Clare Dalton
Chapter title font: Accanthis ADF Std
(Copyright © Arkandis Digital Foundry
under the GNU General Public License V2)

Print ISBN 978-1-77369-777-2
Ebook ISBN 978-1-77369-778-9

Golden Meteorite Press
103 11919 82 St NW
Edmonton, AB T5B 2W3
www.goldenmeteoritepress.com

Segments

Introduction   9

Manifest Destiny   13

A Long Journey West   25

Cannibalism at Alder Creek   37

Demographic Analysis   43

Conclusion   53

References: 55

Introduction

Current research into the Donner Party enables us to separate fact from fiction in this highly sensationalized story. Media enthusiasm for the gory details at the time issued the impression to the general public of a group trapped in the mountains, snowed in without adequate supplies or warm clothing, facing starvation and hypothermia. The story is a sympathetic one of settlers looking for a better life, beset by a series of calamities concluding in a nightmare scenario that played out just a few miles short of their destination. Difficult decisions had to be made by survivors, including the impossible calculus of parents over which children were strong enough to attempt to walk out, if an adult should attempt to seek rescue while leaving their children behind, and when to self-rescue and abandon family members who were too weak to move when opportunity presented itself.

Some of the survivors spent the rest of their lives running from what they were forced to do to survive, others embraced their fame and did not shy away from sharing their stories. Most, however, set about building new lives for themselves and appear to have simply wanted to move on. For others, their reputations were permanently damaged by the events of the winter of 1846-1847, demonized in the media and by enthusiastic rescuers who were happy to spread gossip depicting them as ghoulish cannibals addicted to consuming human flesh. The drama of these stories has established a warped and disjointed image of the Donner Party in the public imagination that persists to this day.

The truth of the Donner Party is far murkier than is popularly portrayed. The obsession of the public with the shocking idea of cannibalism perhaps lends to sensationalism before a single word has been written or spoken about the events, and in looking for a simple and orderly interpretation of the world many people prefer narratives of good and evil to those of frightened, imperfect, complicated humans trapped in extreme scenarios. Upon closer examination, however, that is precisely what is seen in this chapter of history. As unpleasant as it may be, the Donner Party is less a window into tragic and isolated events from the past and more a mirror of the human will to survive. These travelers who found themselves stuck in a deadly and impossible situation were forced to engage in the complicated calculus of survival. Where to prioritize their individual needs over others, what risks and actions to take in securing food, shelter, and communication with the outside world. For parents and spouses, to focus their energy on helping their loved ones who were strong and healthy in their escape, or to wait with the sick and the dying in the hope that their condition would improve by the time more rescuers arrived. In the case of Tamzene Donner, who had sent her children away in the care of others to remain behind with her husband, George Donner, who was too ill to walk himself out. She did this not because she believed his condition would improve if only she could help care for him, it was quite clear he was beyond all hope of ever leaving Alder Creek; her choice was to remain with him to ensure he did not die alone (Rarick, 2009). In that complicated calculus she should have known after so many months trapped in that place that she was growing weaker herself, and staying with him likely meant signing her own death warrant. This is in contrast to Philippine Zimmerman, wife of Lewis Keseberg, who chose to take their child and leave with one of the rescue parties while her husband was injured and unable to join them on the long journey to safety (Voeller, 2009).

There is considerable difference in the way this journey is thought of, as well. In the minds of many it is a story of struggle, resilience, horrors, and tragic consequences in the simple search for opportunity and new beginnings in the West. To many Indigenous peoples, however, the story of the Donner Party carries similar character to many colonial stories; it is a tale of greed, expansionism, and tragedy stemming from people driving themselves headlong into a dangerous situation without a proper understanding of their surroundings (Schablitsky, 2012). It is easy to make that connection when the Indigenous perspective is taken into account. The Donner Party were visitors to the area around Truckee Lake, they had no desire to stay there and did not have proper clothing or skills to survive the extreme conditions at those altitudes. Even the tribe that traditionally inhabits the regions migrates to more forgiving climates for the winter months, with only small parties periodically visiting the area to hunt (Schablitsky, 2012). These people bore witness to the horrors that befell the Donner Party, did what little they could to help, but ultimately were driven off by the settlers, opting to observe from a distance and take no active role in the success or failure of the group.

This book will look at some of the current research into the prevalence of cannibalism by party members, particularly at the Alder Creek site with much archaeological evidence being hard pressed to identify any definitive proof of cannibalism at either of the camps occupied by party members. Statistical analysis into the demographic outcomes of the party also offers interesting insights into the age groups, social connections, and gender dynamics that appear to have significantly tipped the scales in favour of married adult women to survive in such a challenging scenario. Furthermore, this book will review the social dynamics of the Donner Party and how a lack of social cohesion and strong leadership may have been a significant factor in the outcome of their journey.

Manifest Destiny

The idea of Manifest Destiny originates in the years immediately before the Donner Party departed on their journey west. It is the expansionist idea that the United States was ordained by God to spread democracy and capitalism to the rest of the continent, and is generally understood to spread these concepts through direct territorial control. In other words, Manifest Destiny is the idea that the United States is a nation smiled upon by a higher power, and that its borders should expand to include as much of North America as possible. At the time, most of the territory to the west of the Great Lakes was unclaimed by the U.S government, and still generally occupied by the traditional Indigenous populations that had lived in those places for millenia. As for California, it was still part of Mexico but the U.S would go to war with Mexico in that period as well and ultimately take control over California, making it a U.S state (Rarick, 2009). The mythology and language of Manifest Destiny was still in its infancy when the Donner Party planned their journey, and they do not appear to have been concerned with whether California was part of Mexico or America, their primary interest was in the opportunity presented by the rapidly growing economy and the free land that was being offered to settlers who agreed to create functioning farms that were important to bolster the region and expand the capacity for a more advanced and populace economy. While it does not appear as though members of the Donner Party were heading to California specifically with the idea of Manifest Destiny in their hearts, they were nevertheless part of the shifting demographics that made the American annexation of California possible. A group of mostly english-speaking settlers who had lived if not their entire lives then at least for many years in the United States, moving to claim land and participate in the economy of a Mexican territory that was in the sights of the United States. There was already a substantial American population in California that ultimately would spark a rebellion and lead the effort to take California from Mexico. So the Donners, if not actively considering the idea of expanding the borders of the United States, were nevertheless participants in the foundational movements that we now refer to in shorthand as Manifest Destiny.

There are elements to Manifest Destiny that may be unfamiliar in the modern context. It is commonly understood that North America was viewed as unclaimed and untamed regardless of the Indigenous civilizations that existed; this idea of expansionism enjoys broad awareness. What may not be so well understood is the element of Christian Nationalism that existed at the heart of Manifest Destiny. It was not as simple as spreading democracy and capitalism across the continent and expanding the borders of the United States, there was an urgency added by what would today be considered fanatical Christian elements as well. John O'Sullivan first published the term Manifest Destiny in 1845 in an article aimed at justifying the U.S annexation of the Republic of Texas (Wilsey, 2017). O'Sullivan had been promoting American expansion in his writings since the early 1830's, with a clear bend toward various elements of Protestant theology in justifying his vision of spreading Christianity along with democracy and capitalism; O'Sullivan, in other words, felt as if liberalism were the ordained ideology of the Christian God. This aggressive religious element to nation-building was not unprecedented but it did signify an expansion of religious power over U.S policy at the time. It should be unfamiliar in the modern context because there is a strong devotion to the separation of church and state, and while territorial expansion is unfamiliar but understood, the degree of overt religious motivation in Manifest Destiny is particularly notable. This becomes particularly clear when we consider that separation of church and state were supposed to be ideals embraced in the founding of the United States, as a response to their rejection of traditional authority structures upheld by the colonial powers in England. Part of the rejection of the King was a rejection of government sanctioned religion, and an important part of early liberal thinking was the redefinition of what was considered the realm of personal and private. The idea of liberty, or freedom from government interference in personal lives included the concept of the rule of law, which is an important departure from feudal government, but also the concepts of private property, social mobility, and religious freedom were central ideas. It is important to remember that many internal contradictions existed in early liberalism, and factors such as freedom of religion were not embraced by all. So while separation of church and state was an important concept in liberalism and the United States constitution, there did exist some powerful interests within liberalism that disagreed with the idea. Therefore, while the overt Christian Nationalist element of Manifest Destiny appears to contradict some of the core values of early liberalism, it was not a particularly unusual discrepancy in the political climate at the time. In fact, the religious element may have successfully inspired much of the public enthusiasm for the massive expansion of the United States borders.

Stuckey (2011) argues that the Donner Party became the singular cultural touchpoint for western expansion, and despite the horrific end it actually encouraged more settlers to attempt the journey. In this way, the Donner Party serves as a cautionary tale for how to complete the journey successfully, rather than a discouraging one. To highlight this argument, she references a famous letter from one of the children who survived the tragedy to one of their cousins urging settlers to hurry along and don't bother with shortcuts, and even after all they had seen, the child claimed not to have any regrets and encouraged others to come (Stuckey, 2011).

Stuckey (2011) goes on to argue that the Donner Party is a viable touchstone by which the development of American identity can be measured during this period of western expansion. One of the important elements the Donner Party highlights is erasure. America is an important experiment in democracy, and constructing a nation without the baggage of a highly developed and entrenched class system resulting from hundreds of years of feudal rule. This experiment is portrayed as being pure and without cost, but to accomplish that image it is important to erase the experiences of the Indigenous peoples from whom all American territory was taken. If North America is portrayed as an empty landmass waiting to be conquered and civilized, rather than a place with an existing network of highly developed societies already, it is easy to view the American experiment as a pure exercise. Something that thoughtful people engaged in without taking anything away from anybody else, making it a pure and wholesome exercise in attempting to build a better nation.

Erasure can be observed in a number of very successful and organized efforts that are easily mistaken by casual observers as being unintentional, perfectly innocent portrayals of history and geography. The long-term viability of colonization requires that the recorded history of a place begins with the colonization, and we see this clearly playing out on the North American continent. No pre-columbian history is taught or discussed about the place, and while the broad discourse does concede that people existed here when colonial powers arrived, they are portrayed as savages possessed of neither advanced technology nor worthy societies. Another important element in erasure is the colonization of language with regards to geography. Traditional names are removed and replaced by names assigned to places by colonizers (Stuckey, 2011). This is observable with the Donner Party with regards to Truckee Lake and Truckee Pass where they became trapped. The original name was given to those places in honour of a local Paiute (Stuckey, 2011). Following the tragic events of the Donner Party, however, those places have since been renamed Donner Lake and Donner Pass respectively (Rarick, 2009). Here we can see a clear example of how the naming of locations helps to erase the non-colonial history of a place.

The second way in which Stuckey (2011) argues the Donner Party represents the development of American identity is the triumph of society over nature even in extreme conditions. This survival of civilization is paramount, and since there were a significant number of survivors it can be used as an example of how God wants the United States to succeed, thus we see the concept of American Identity in this time period closely merging with the values of Manifest Destiny. There is an indominability of spirit implied in the survival of many members of the Donner Party. If they can live through extreme cold for nearly six months, perhaps even viewing the deaths of their comrades as necessary in ultimately providing the calories required to complete the journey, how can anybody argue God was not on their side?

When viewed in such terms, the Donner Party becomes a call to action for the continued expansion of the United States across the continent, regardless of whether the members of the party intended to serve the interests of one particular nation. Part of the mythology of Manifest Destiny is the idea that there is fortune to be found just over the horizon, all one needs to do is seek it out. So in serving their self-interest and turning their eyes westward, the Donner Party became a symbol that was easily claimed by proponents of Manifest Destiny. This can be interpreted as a 'no press is bad press' mentality from the proponents of expansion. The infamy of the Donner Party was precisely what made the events of their journey so commonly known; it only took cleverly managed messaging to turn those horrific events into the inspirational cautionary tale of the virtues of American civilization that it ultimately became.

The third element of American Identity that Stuckey (2011) identifies in the Donner Party is the triumph of the community; this was the narrative used to inspire and sustain frontier communities. This theme of competing values between the individual and collective is seen consistently through American history and remains spirited to this day. The contrast between individualism and community creates tension in the narrative of the Donner Party, and popular discourse surrounding the characters often glorifies the contributions of individuals who made decisions benefitting the collective, while punishing those who acted in self-interest. The contrast between the characters of Tamzene Donner and Lewis Keseberg is fertile ground for this analysis.

Tamzene Donner collaborated with her neighbors to ensure care for her children when it was their time to go along with the rescue parties, but made the decision to stay with her husband, George Donner, who was too sick to go along. She did not want him to die alone, and opted to care for him in his final weeks instead of participating in rescue herself, a decision that ended up being a death sentence for her. Tamzene was with her husband when he died, but she had been significantly weakened in that time as well. She spent her final burst of energy making the kilometers-long journey from Alder Creek to Truckee Lake, where Lewis Keseberg was the only remaining survivor, before she also succumbed to some combination of exposure and starvation (Rarick, 2009). For making this choice, she is often assigned a positive designation in the narrative. Her choices were social ones, they contributed to the community in one way or another, right up to sacrificing her own life to preserve even a minimum level of community for George Donner on his deathbed.

Lewis Keseberg, on the other hand, was the last survivor rescued from the Donner Party. He admitted freely to committing cannibalism to survive, and the party that rescued him was relentless in their character assassination. They portrayed him as a self-serving ghoul, delighting in the consumption of human flesh. There was also some drama over his hiding of a cache of valuables that he claimed were entrusted to him by Tamzene Donner in her final hours. He claimed she gave him what remained of the family money so that he could hide it, and come back later to retrieve it and ensure the money benefitted her surviving children. One final act of community from Tamzene, but that cast further doubt on the character of Lewis Keseberg. If he lived up to that supposed promise, Keseberg would have been serving a community interest. His rescue party, on the other hand, was actually a salvage party that had secured an agreement with the government of California to retrieve all valuables related to the Donner Party in exchange for a cut, to ensure that at least some of the valuables would benefit the survivors. They accused Keseberg of interfering with their operation by refusing to give up the Donner gold, and even threatened to kill him before he relented and revealed the location of the cache. When they returned to safety with Keseberg they accused him of wanting to keep the gold for himself, and exaggerated his cannibalism. This portrayal paints Keseberg as an individualist who survived and planned to profit in the future by feeding off what belonged to his community (Rarick, 2009). The difference in narrative is clear. Tamzene Donner was a hero, self-sacrificing for communal benefit. Lewis Keseberg was a villain, a self-serving cannibal whose interest was transparently for his individual benefit.

Finally, the fourth element of American identity that Stuckey (2011) discusses is the triumph of democracy. Wagon trains, including the Donner Party, were democratic exercises. These communities on the move elected leaders, made big decisions by vote, laid out and agreed to rules they would follow once they had left the borders of the United States, and when those rules were seriously broken the perpetrators were placed under arrest and given a trial by judge and jury, even being entitled to legal defense (Rarick, 2009). In many ways, the democracy seen in the wagon trains demonstrated a system of suffrage far advanced from the classical lliberal approach of the United States at the time. Democracy in America still only broadly gave political power to white male landowners, but on the wagon trains everyone had to walk just as far as everyone else. This led to a less formal decision making process that gave a voice to all members of the community, although with the politics and individual biases in-tact. This means the democracy of the wagon trains was more inclusive than was typically seen in nation states at the time, but should not be mistaken for the concept of total equity in the political system.

The way the Donner Party became a symbol for democracy was by offering a powerful warning to wagon trains and the frontier community more broadly about the importance of mobility. America was a nation on the move, but the only way to achieve the power and status that Manifest Destiny promised was to remain in motion (Stuckey, 2011). Thus, to become trapped as the Donner Party did at Truckee Lake became a warning. Democracy, social order, common purpose, these things all fell apart for the Donner Party when they stopped moving. It's important to recognize here that this argument was an effective propaganda tool in the orthodoxy of Manifest Destiny, but the concepts of community, mutual cooperation, and democracy had long since disintegrated within the Donner Party before they became stuck. When the storm rolled in from the West as the settlers were passing through Alder Creek and Truckee Lake, the party had separated into three distinct groups centered around family structures, which is why the Donner family was separated from the rest of the party and trapped in a second location (Rarick, 2009). Even though the larger group at Truckee Lake separated into four separate cabins, they were not concerned nor interested in working together because they understood that supplies were critically low and they didn't have the right clothing or equipment for a winter stay. The fateful decision to take the Hastings cutoff had already proven to be an expensive disaster in terms of supplies, energy, and perhaps most importantly: time (Rarick, 2009). In the months leading up to their entrapment, the Donner Party had experienced fractures and social divisions stemming from their frustrations over the lack of progress.

A few of the relevant concepts from this fourth characteristic can be observed in the banishment of James Reed. In October of 1846 Reed got into an argument with John Snyder over two of their wagons becoming entangled. The argument became heated, and Snyder struck Reed over the forehead with the hilt of his bullwhip hard enough to draw blood. In the same moment, Reed drove his knife into Snyders chest, dealing a fatal wound. Snyder died a short time later, surrounded by party members. A court was struck to deal with the issue. Under normal circumstances George Donner would have presided over the hearing but his group was a day ahead on the trail. Lewis Keseberg argued that Reed should be hanged for his crime, while others defended Reed with conflicting eyewitness testimony claiming it was an accident. Even those arguing for Reed's guilt would begrudgingly have to concede it was a hot-blooded crime, not premeditated murder. The court reached a compromise. There would be no death penalty for Reed, but he was to be banished. The next morning Reed took his horse and left the party without food or even a hunting rifle; his family stayed with the group (Rarick, 2009). Reed's daughter was able to sneak away and provide him with some supplies and the means to hunt for himself a few days later, but it was well understood that being banished to continue on the trail alone was as good as a death sentence for Reed. Ironically, Reed safely reached California and was spared the tragedy to come, and was even instrumental in organizing and leading rescue efforts later.

Reed's argument with Snyder was the result of a breakdown in the social cohesion of the party. The separation of the wagon train into multiple groups spread days apart on the trail also signals this, thus George Donner was not present to sit in judgment over Reed. The court reached a compromise solution that effectively ended the matter without further division, and Reed played a central role in helping rescue the survivors, signifying the success of the democratic characteristic identified by Stuckey (2011). So on this final point it is possible to recognize the internal contradictions present in the actual events of the Donner Party, while appreciating the elements that can be cherry-picked to support the Donner Party as an effective symbol for Manifest Destiny.

The concept of Manifest Destiny amounted to an ambitious and wildly successful public relations campaign to justify the expansion of American ideology, political power, territorial claims, and Christian nationalism by inspiring the public with a common purpose that was claimed to be ordained by God (Wilsey, 2017). Furthermore, Manifest Destiny was an important concept in building an American identity that was necessary to inspire the spread of the young nation across the continent and emerge as a major world power. The Donner Party came to be a symbol of Manifest Destiny and a complicated marker for the ideal characteristics of American identity that were being proposed including erasure of Indigenous heritage, the triumph of society over nature, the triumph of community over hardship, and the triumph of democracy including a warning that a community, whether small or massive, was doomed if it stopped moving (Stuckey, 2011). Diving deeply into these exercises pulls back the curtain on some interesting contradictions, as can be expected when such a complicated and prolonged tragedy is boiled down to being little more than a symbolic effort to justify what amounts to a political slogan. At the heart of Manifest Destiny rests a stream of Christian nationalism that today would be considered fanatical, and was out of step with the American commitment to the separation of church and state. Erasure of Indigenous heritage was important to give the impression that expanding U.S borders across the continent was a pure and righteous act, as opposed to the violent and tragic reality the exercise created for millions of Indigenous peoples who had already been decimated and oppressed by colonial activities for centuries at that point. The triumph of society is almost laughable considering the human cost of the events of that winter at Truckee Lake, and the lasting trauma and social stigma it created for the survivors. Triumph of community is complicated as well, being far more gray than black and white because of course the people stranded in the Sierra Nevada were not a community of angels and demons, they were people with conflicting interests, scarcity of resources, and fear. There are examples of personal sacrifice to benefit the community, and there are examples of selfish acts as well; all are difficult to judge from the outside because a person honestly cannot say what choices they would have made. And in the aftermath, depictions of the characters were often skewed in service of this narrative of triumph of the community; it was necessary to assign angels and demons to the story while disregarding the fact that real people were being characterized and fictionalized. And finally, the concept of democracy was also highlighted as a virtue of the Donner Party, and their entrapment in the mountains being blamed for the breakdown of democratic norms among their party. Here again when examined more closely, we find a far more complicated reality. The party was experiencing significant social breakdown for months prior to their being trapped, but the public relations exercise of building an American identity that embraces expansionism and Christian nationalism does not have time for such a complicated reality.

To make the Donner Party an effective vehicle to communicate the virtues of Manifest Destiny and the identity characteristics therein, it was necessary to gloss over the complicated reality of the events. Individuals were recast as simple caricatures, events cherry-picked, and Indigenous peoples painted over. The great American experiment was evolving and it needed its own mythology. The Donner Party presented an excellent opportunity to create such a mythology, containing elements of heroics, cowardice, virtues, and warning.

A Long Journey West

The journey began at Independence, Missouri on the 11th of May, 1846. It was a late start for the Donner Party, who initially planned to join a larger wagon train that set out in April. It is unclear what caused their delay, but there was not yet any cause for alarm; the journey took between four and six months on average, getting a late start should have made the party nervous but it was not cause to call the adventure off (Rarick, 2009). The idea was to make a hard push at the start to catch up to the larger group; this would enable the Donner Party relative safety in numbers from the dangers of the vast western territories. A larger community of travellers allowed for greater security, a more forgiving economic reality, and hopefully a deeper pool would contain better leadership potential. All essential pieces of the puzzle when attempting to navigate the Oregon Trail.

The Donners were just one of the families in the party of nearly 90 people, but the numbers fluctuated and it was common for individuals or even families to separate from the group for various reasons, sometimes joining up again after a time. The patriarch of the Donner family, George Donner, was elected midway through the journey to lead the group (Rarick, 2009), thus the ordeal bears his family name.

The party numbers also fluctuated due to birth and death. Sarah Keyes, mother to Margaret Reed, joined the party despite being roughly 70 years old. The journey routinely resulted in the deaths of strong women half her age, but Keyes may have been willing to take the trip precisely because she was advanced in age and already quite sick with consumption, which was probably tuberculosis (Rarick, 2009). Her only living family was moving to the other side of the continent, and with not much time left it can be understood that she might have wanted to spend the time she had left as close to them as possible. Just a few weeks into the journey, Keyes died. She had confessed a few days earlier to her son-in-law that the journey had sapped what little strength she had left. Her death was not unexpected; she experienced a long decline and had stopped eating for several days prior to her end.

At that point in their journey, the party was stopped at Big Blue River. They needed to cross but recent rains had raised the water level and made it too dangerous to attempt. While they waited, trees were cut and a casket constructed. The party conducted a funeral procession and held a ceremony for Keyes before laying her to rest on a hilltop. The party was down one member, but around that time a baby was born so the Donner Party had the same number of people as the day they left despite experiencing the death of one of their members (Rarick, 2009). It was not uncommon on wagon trains for pregnant women to give birth during the journey.

The journey had been relatively slow and marked by multiple minor misfortunes, but there was not yet cause for alarm by July 12th when they were crossing Wyoming. One of the things that can be said of travel along the Oregon trail was that it was better to start early and finish early, and groups that pushed themselves in the early days while they were still on the grass rich prairies were making a sort of investment in their journey that would pay off handsomely later on. The farther west along the trail they went, the more challenging the conditions for the wagons and the livestock they brought with them. For some members of the Donner Party, it was maddening that in their journey through the easier early regions had been characterized by short days and even weekends of rest; at every turn, the Donner Party were choosing not to push themselves too hard or make the investments that would have been so beneficial and could even have prevented the disaster from happening at all (Rarick, 2009).

As they proceeded west, the group found themselves traveling through areas with less and less water, more difficult terrain for their wagons to cross, and less grass to keep their livestock strong and happy (Rarick, 2009). None of this should have been a surprise, they were far from the first settlers to make the journey and the geography of North America, particularly along the Oregon Trail was well understood. Perhaps it was a case of wishful thinking, of believing what lay ahead could not possibly be worse than the difficulty they were already experiencing on the trail. One reason used to justify the leisurely early pace was that it was best not to push the livestock too hard, the animals were one of the most important resources for the group and their care was always at the forefront of the settlers' minds. It was an ingenious strategy employed by travelers on the trail, bringing livestock in large numbers would serve to give the party fresh meat and milk along the way, and the animals largely care for themselves by grazing and drinking, generally finding it easier to live off the land than people. There is work associated with herding the animals and keeping track of them, but these tasks prove relatively minor when stacked up against having to travel for as much as 16 hours per day and then hunt for food in unfamiliar territory. Keeping animals with their wagon train in their hundreds presented a great bit of efficiency. Moreover, a lucky group would arrive in either Oregon or California with most animals in-tact, and they could be sold for a profit at their destinations to offset the costs of undertaking such a journey.

Taking animals along with them did not mean the parties never opted to hunt. After all, the ability to sell the animals for a profit at their destination was a powerful motivator to preserve as many animals as possible through the journey, so hunting was a common activity on the trail (Rarick, 2009). Many men in the wagon trains including on the Donner Party walked along with their rifles cocked and loaded in case they came across some wildlife in their daily travels, and this was frequently the case. This was a further efficiency, if a deer or bison could be taken on the trail it saved not only the livestock traveling with the party, but displaced the need for a hunting party to be conducted when the group stopped for the night. Typically when an animal was taken down by a party member along the route, they would butcher their kill right there as the rest of the party continued on and the fresh meat would be carried at a faster pace to catch up to the wagons of the family to whom the hunter belonged. Luckily, the wagon trains did not travel at torrential speed. Their rate of travel was dictated by the oxen pulling their carts, which move at the near glacial pace of barely 2 km per hour in ideal conditions, less so when the landscape is harsh.

The wagons were particularly bedeviled by any positive or negative grade in the trail (Rarick, 2009). Being loaded up with tons of goods and supplies, every degree of incline in the trail exponentially increases the difficulty of hauling the weight. On level terrain only two oxen were needed to move a train, but up a steep grade it was sometimes necessary to unhook the animals from a dozen other carts to move a single one up a hill. The process would need to be repeated for every wagon in the train while other families and wagons waited their turn. Progress in such circumstances would have been infuriatingly slow, taking days to advance the entire party just a few hundred meters.

Perhaps more risky were the declines, however. At that point most wagons had no breaking mechanism, so there was no good solution to preventing wagons from running over their oxen and rolling uncontrolled down a hill (Rarick, 2009). If the decline was steep enough to overwhelm the animals, settlers would sometimes use what was referred to as a land anchor to create some drag and prevent the oxen from being overwhelmed by the weight of the cart pushing on them from behind. The concept is precisely as crude as it sounds, and worked with mixed results. A large log would be attached to a long rope, the leading end of which was tied to the back of a wagon. As the log dragged along the ground it would create resistance that would hopefully help maintain a manageable rate of travel for the oxen and prevent the cart from rolling out of control. This strategy, coupled with the appearance of settlers' wagons at a distance with their canvas covers lent them the nickname of land schooners (Rarick, 2009).

On July 12 a rider delivered a message to the Donner Party as they traveled through Wyoming. It was a form letter addressed to any travelers on the Oregon Trail from a man named Lansford Hastings, advertising a shortcut that he claimed would save them weeks of travel time by diverting south through what is now Utah and Nevada, rather than the traditional route to California that followed the Oregon Trail north into Idaho before splitting south into Nevada. The new route was called the Hastings Cutoff, and if it was as good as advertised it would see the party arrive in California well before winter set in. In his letter, Hastings promised to meet settlers wishing to try his new route at Fort Bridger, deep in the southwest corner of Wyoming. Fort Bridger was not on the main Oregon Trail, it was along a minor detour to the south of the main route just to the east of the Wasatch mountain range. The fort represented the fork in the road. Travel directly west and they would be on Hastings' shortcut, travel north and west and they would be on the well populated and traveled Oregon Trail. It was a risky option, taken on the word of a stranger, but the party decided to risk it. Frustrations over their slow progress likely played a role in the choice to take the word of a stranger and an untested shortcut, but he did claim to have found a faster way through and the party was feeling pressure to make up time. The Hastings Cutoff would be their route.

They got one final opportunity to change their mind when they reached Fort Bridger and discovered Lansford Hastings had been there, but had already left with another party. There was a strong desire to take the shortcut, but now they would be attempting the more risky route without a guide. Some, including James Reed, argued they would not necessarily be without a guide, the other party could not be that far ahead and evidence of their travel could be observed along the way. All the party needed to do was follow the footsteps of the group ahead and they would be fine.

Journalist Edwin Bryant had moved with the Donner Party for several weeks in their approach to Wyoming, but became frustrated with the slow pace and opted to strike out on his own. Bryant reached Fort Bridger a week before the rest of the party, and he knew they were considering the Hastings Cutoff. Hastings had already left when Bryant arrived, but he did observe the start of the cutoff and was concerned it was too rugged and challenging for the wagons of the Donner Party. Before opting to continue along the traditional route of the Oregon Trail, Bryant left letters at the fort for when the Donner Party arrived warning them not to go that route (Rarick, 2009). Unfortunately, the owner of the post, felt it was in his interest if settlers used the Hastings Cutoff because his location would be an important spot for the purchase of supplies; he hid the letters from the Donners when they arrived and told them the cutoff was an easy trip, devoid of hard terrain or hostile Indigenous peoples, with easy access to grazing lands and water the entire way. Additionally, he told them the cutoff would save them 560 km on their journey to California.

Between the false information from the fort and Reed's argument that the trail would be visible by the wagon train ahead of them, the decision was made. The Donner Party voted to take the Hastings Cutoff. To their misfortune, Lansford Hastings proved to be an ambitious man; he was eager to make a name for himself. The Hastings Cutoff was one of many endeavors he employed to write his name into the history books; he also aspired to overthrow Mexican rule of California and dreamt of being elected governor of the newest American territory. What Hastings left out of his communications to the Donners and all the other settlers was that he had not actually traveled this supposed shortcut. The territory through which he proposed they move was an unknown quantity to the colonial community, and there was no way for him to know whether this was passable territory for wagon trains populated with children, livestock, and tons of goods loaded on clumsy wagons.

In reality, the proposed route for the Hastings Cutoff is arguably one of the worst possible places that wagon trains could attempt to cross. Immediately, settlers were required to blaze a trail through the heart of the Wasatch mountain range. It was difficult enough traveling up or downhill on established trails that were found on the main route used by settlers, but Hastings route was entirely untested so the party was required to scout passable trails and cut trees to make room for their wagons before they could even begin worrying about the tedious work of hitching multiple teams of oxen to a single wagon and ferrying the animals up and down hills to move the entire train along. They immediately had difficulty identifying the path taken by the party ahead of them because it had been several weeks since they moved through the area. Only occasionally did the Donner Party land on some territory that had already been broken in.

Once they cleared the Wasatch range, the party moved along the south shore of Great Salt Lake, and here the difficulties truly began (Rarick, 2009). There was no fresh water accessible for the livestock or people for a long distance. Upon reaching the other side of the lake they were presented with further difficulty, they needed to cross the Great Salt Lake Desert. Not only was there no fresh water, but there was no shelter, either and the ground was too soft for easy passage of the wagons. It took multiple days to cross the desert, during which time multiple wagons had to be abandoned, the party fractured into small groups based on their individual rates of travel, scores of livestock died of dehydration, the nights proved to be bitterly cold combined with frequent storms which made the crossing a miserable experience. Members of the party were exhausted and dehydrated, and now at risk of dying of exposure. According to Rarick (2009), they were walking across "one of the most inhospitable places on Earth" (p. 69).

The final leg of the Hastings Cutoff before rejoining the main trail involved a long detour around the Ruby Mountains to avoid the arduous and possibly impossible task of cutting through the middle of yet another mountain range. The decision to take a long detour saved the party any major drama in this last stretch, but also ate up valuable time. It took the Donner Party two months to complete the Hastings Cutoff and incalculable losses of livestock, wagons, and equipment. It is likely that had they stayed on the main trail the entire time, they would have reached the same point on the map as much as a month earlier with their livestock and other assets intact (Rarick, 2009). The ambitions of Hastings had cost the Donner Party dearly, and his diversion is possibly the most significant factor in leading to what came next if for no other reason than the time they wasted picking their way across Utah and into Nevada.

Once back on the main trail, the sense of community within the Donner Party was seriously challenged. This was the period where James Reed killed John Snyder and was banished, and the party had already begun to fracture into smaller family groups because some were able to travel faster than others (Rarick, 2009). This portion of the trail through Nevada is what was warned about when the party began; resources were more scarce. Grass and fresh water were difficult to come by, but not impossible. The result is damage to the social cohesion of a group that had been pushed to the breaking point, and their remaining livestock began to weaken significantly. Family groups grew mistrustful of one another, further contributing to the disintegration of the broader party. As they began their long march into the Sierra Nevada, the Donner Party had become a collection of three or four smaller groups all traveling the same path at the same time, but they were spread out and unfriendly with one another.

The animals had grown so weakened that it was necessary to spare any unnecessary exertion. No party members were allowed to ride on horses or in wagons; items viewed as disposable were discarded. It became so necessary for people to walk that Keseberg ejected the 70 year old Hardcoop from a wagon, telling the man he was expected to walk just like everybody else. After walking until his feet were swollen and bloodied, the elderly man sat down on the side of the trail and refused to go on. At the end of the day, William Eddy noticed Hardcoop was missing and attempted to organize a search party, but the group refused to commit resources to attempt to find and bring him back. Hardcoop was never seen again and is assumed to have died on the side of the road somewhere in Nevada where he sat himself down.

The party settlers melded into nearly a single mass again, although they were still on poor social terms with one another, and their hardship continued. The Graves family lost all their horses, night raids by the local Indigenous population stole and killed around 40 more cattle, and more wagons were abandoned (Rarick, 2009). During their crossing of the final stretch of desert before reaching Truckee River, the Eddy's lost the last of their oxen and were forced to abandon their wagon. Out of food, low on water, the family was forced to walk and other settlers refused to help even the children.

When they reached Truckee River, it must have looked like a miracle of plentiful lush green grass, but there was no time to rest. It was mid October already and the party was now in a race to get across the Sierra Nevada mountain range before the first snow fell. They were under extreme pressure to press on. Charles Stanton, who had left the party to charge ahead to California for fresh supplies several months earlier rejoined them here. He had fresh oxen and supplies, although fairly meager when weighed against nearly 90 other souls in the party but was nevertheless a morale booster. He had also hired two Indigenous men to help with his effort, Luis and Salvador. He was also able to pass on the news that Reed had reached Suttler's Fort in California, very encouraging news that their long journey was almost complete.

Word was the mountain pass did not usually get blocked by snow until mid November, so they should have had enough time to make it through if they did not delay. It is also the case that snowfall in that area is extreme, so once it does begin to fall it creates a dangerous and impossible obstacle. Rarick (2009) writes that when the railway was run through that same pass in the late 1870's is when annual snowfall records began being kept, but the first year the railway opened 24 meters of snow was recorded in the season. Snowfall was likely not quite that extreme in the winter of 1846, but the obstacle was significant all the same.

As the party was deciding whether to rest their cattle or press on immediately, an accidental discharge of William Foster's rifle struck William Pike in the base of the spine. Witnesses described his death as occurring half an hour later after the man had endured indescribable pain (Rarick, 2009). Death by accidental discharge was a fairly common occurrence among settler groups. The popular image of hardy pioneers living independently on the trail is a common misconception; most of these settlers had very little experience in the wild, and their firearms handling skills left much to be desired. Rarick (2009) reports one case where a settler was killed when a rifle was accidentally discharged after the mechanism was caught by a woman's skirt. The death of Pike sobered the party up, and one by one the family groups resumed their journey.

The Donners moved last, and once they did start to travel the rough terrain broke an axle on one of their wagons. It was necessary to fashion a replacement, a process that would burn valuable time. While working on the replacement axle, George Donner cut his hand in what appeared to be a superficial wound (Rarick, 2009). This is why the Donners were so far separated from the rest of the group when everyone was forced to settle in for the winter.

Within a few days, snow began falling. The Breens, Murphy's, Graves' and Reeds were all forced to stop and camp on the east end of Truckee Lake; the pass was blocked by snowfall measuring at least three meters. The Donners were forced to stop at Alder Creek, nearly a dozen kilometers east of Truckee Lake. For the larger group at the lakesite, they built crude cabins with what limited time, resources, and skills they had. Some had just canvas or hide as roofing material, although being buried under so much snow they likely discovered that snow is an excellent insulator and probably did a decent job keeping the inside of their living space relatively warm when they did manage to maintain a fire. The Donners were even more crude with their living arrangements. It seems they tried to continue on the trail for as long as possible, perhaps trying to reach the rest of the party. In the end, they ran out of time and were forced to construct shelter with what little daylight they allowed themselves, perhaps not realizing they would not be able to improve later. The Donners constructed simple tents and what hard shelter they did build was to be used as a cooking area; they were no doubt the least sheltered group that winter (Rarick, 2009).

During the night, a great volume of snow fell that created an entirely new set of problems for the settlers. First, it was impossible to improve on their shelters in snow that deep. Additionally, ini their rush to erect shelter, they neglected to create a centralized location for the cattle, instead allowing the animals to roam free. Under several meters of accumulated snow, it became impossible to find where the animals ended up. As snow continued to fall that winter and food supplies became more scarce, it must have been infuriating to know there were entire animals frozen and preserved under that icy blanket, but there was no way of locating them. For better or for worse, the Donner Party was now trapped. They would not be going anywhere, nobody knew there was an emergency unfolding. No help would be coming.

Relief efforts, once they did begin, proved to be maddeningly difficult. The trouble was that there was still 200 kilometers of difficult terrain to cross before reaching the next settlement. Victims of the tragedy must be strong enough to walk themselves out because there were simply no tools available to transport them out any other way. When rescuers did begin efforts, they quickly discovered no pack animals were able to traverse the snow, so rescue supplies were limited to what could be carried by men. The men had to carry enough to get themselves to Truckee Lake, and then walk back out, and that does not yet account for even one gram of supplies for the starving and desperate people they're attempting to rescue (Rarick, 2009).

For this reason, there were multiple rescue efforts that were carried out after the emergency became known, but sometimes the party was left unattended for weeks between rescues and the difficult calculus of deciding who was strong enough to make the journey began. Many died attempting to walk out, even with rescuers. Many more died at the lake camp and Alder Creek between rescue efforts.

George Donner was one of the last to die. The cut he sustained in October while fixing his wagon became infected, and then in the unhygienic conditions of his shelter at Alder Creek it festered. After months of sitting idle in his shelter and being cared for by his wife Tamzene, his entire arm had become swollen and paralyzed. He was too weak to move himself around the cabin, let alone make the long difficult walk down out of the mountains.

In the end, roughly half of the members of the Donner Party died. There were many factors that led to the disaster, and the enormity of human suffering experienced in the winter of 1846-47 is difficult to comprehend. Whether the Donners are to be viewed as simple settlers seeking a better life, or conquerors engaging in an exercise of greed is beyond the scope of this book. But what is clear is that bad luck is too small a word to describe the many problems endured by the Donner Party. They were inexperienced at living on the land. Unprepared for the difficulties that laid ahead of them. Unwilling to push themselves early on. Tempers flared, accidents happened, relationships broke down, and finally, mother nature locked them into a desperate situation.

Cannibalism at Alder Creek

Accounts of cannibalism on the Donner Party are varied, sometimes nakedly unreliable, and often conflicting. Most newspaper articles at the time were heavily sensationalized, clearly more interested in selling newspapers than they were in communicating facts. There are also the reports filed by the various rescue parties claiming to have seen the evidence, but some of the rescuers were motivated by the attention they received and were thus incentivized to exaggerate their claims as well. There was also a very public spat between the final survivor, Lewis Keseberg, and the salvage party that rescued him. The salvagers famously claimed Keseberg told them he preferred consuming human meat to California beef, which was excitedly printed by newspaper editors to great public interest. Keseberg on the other hand, admitted to being forced to cannibalize other party members to survive, but also lamented the horrific nature of the exercise. And he was hostile toward the final party that visited Truckee Lake, because they were not rescuers but salvagers, having signed an agreement with California officials allowing them to keep a significant portion of any cash, gold, or other valuables recovered, while a small portion would be passed along to the survivors of the ordeal (Rarick, 2009).

When the salvagers reached Truckee Lake in April of 1847, they found all dead with the exception of Keseberg. The final survivor claimed the party had little interest in rescuing him, but wasted no time in threatening his life unless he revealed the location of a stash of gold hidden by Tamzene Donner shortly before her death. His story was that Donner entrusted him with the gold to ensure the surviving Donner children would be cared for, and he was reluctant to reveal it to this group of salvagers because their agreement would allow them to keep much of the gold for themselves. The salvagers, on the other hand, accused Keseberg of not only trying to keep the Donner gold hidden so that he might return and keep the entire sum for himself, but also of murdering Tamzene Donner and cannibalising her immediately. It should be noted, however, that Tamzene Donner's body was later found without any evidence of harm, she appeared to have died of starvation and exhaustion. In the end, facing threats of violence, Keseberg revealed the location of the Donner gold and was escorted down out of the mountains by the party; he maintained that despite his weakened state, the group offered him no aid in descending the pass because the party members were so heavily laden with gold, silver, jewelry, and other valuables stripped from the bodies and cabins of the camp (Rarick, 2009). In the case of Keseberg, it is not difficult to see the logic and conflict in both sides of the story. With no objective observer to report on what happened, speculation is the only tool available in the search for truth.

Following his rescue, Keseberg became something of a social pariah. He was often threatened with violence, and one of the members of the salvage party in particular continued his public attacks on Keseberg to the point where Keseberg brought a defamation suit against the man. The court found in Keseberg's favour, but awarded him just $1 in damages. The reason the court gave was that yes, Keseberg was the victim of defamation, however, the jury found the slanderers had broken tarnished goods (Rarick, 2009). Keseberg's public character was so damaged by the events of the Donner party that he was apparently fair game for public mockery.

Among the survivors of the party there were some who openly discussed their part in cannibalism, others refused to speak of it, some denied their involvement at all. There exist a great many primary sources to confirm that cannibalism did occur. For modern academics, however, the issue of locating scientific evidence to prove the claims has been more difficult. Some researchers who have examined both the Truckee (Donner) Lake and Alder Creek campsites have failed to locate any physical evidence at all. Other studies have found potential evidence, but could not conclusively determine the extent of cannibalism due to environmental factors in the area (Dixon et al., 2010). The question is not whether cannibalism occurred, but determining the extent has shown to be very challenging.

Dixon et al. (2010) conducted a study of bone fragments from the Alder Creek site where the Donner family spent the fateful winter. They recognize that there is a different social and demographic makeup between the Alder Creek and Lake sites. The Lake site consisted of the bulk of the party, with several families located between three separate cabins where the members bartered and traded various materials and items and cooked their meals at separate cooksites. The Alder Creek camp contained just one family, and Dixon et al. (2010) were able to identify the single communal hearth site where food was prepared and shared. In their research they analyzed a number of bone fragments and were able to identify tissue from livestock, horses, dogs, rodents, and wild animals, but with no conclusive evidence of human remains. But in their analysis of animal samples there is interesting information to be gleaned.

For example, analysis has shown that bone fragments from the cooking area were chopped, sawed, heated, burned, and boiled (Dixon et al., 2010, Kelly, 2006). This is characteristic of extremely thorough food preparation, boiling bones in particular is the most destructive and least productive activity in food preparation. Boiling is a technique that yields calories from grease and vitamins and minerals in relatively low levels, and is typically the last thing done in processing a food source. Survival cannibalism is often looked on as a fairly predictable process where the amount of effort put into extracting calories is directly proportional to how desperate the scenario is. To illustrate, the first stage of survival cannibalism typically involves dehumanizing the body while the starving person wrestles with the psychological difficulty of the act they are committing. They also target the cheapest calories to harvest, which is large muscle groups and certain organs; these parts have the added benefit of being easily dehumanized when it is time for consumption. If lack of food resources persists, the survivor becomes more desperate and less concerned with dehumanization, and becomes more thorough in their consumption of the corpse including parts that they would not typically look at as being food. The final stage in survival cannibalism involves cracking open and boiling bones to extract every last possible calorie.

A key observation from Dixon et al (2010) is that while they were unable to confirm any human bone fragments at the Alder Creek hearth, the animal bone fragments were varied and extremely advanced in their processing. The Donner family was reduced to consuming dogs and rodents, going so far as to boil the bones even while there was conceivably easy access to human corpses. One conclusion that might be drawn from this observation is that the people at Alder Creek went to the greatest possible lengths to avoid or delay cannibalism.

The oral histories of the Indigenous people who live in the area also confirm that members of the Donner Party were observed consuming human remains. The Northern Washoe (*wel mel ti*) traditionally occupy the territory of Donner Lake and Alder Creek, in fact one of their village sites is just a few kilometers from where the settlers were trapped; although their custom was to spend their winters at lower, more forgiving altitudes, travel through the area on snowshoes was still common (Schablitsky, 2012). In their account, the *wel mel ti* tell of a group of travelers who spent the winter in the area but were unprepared. They claim to have tried to help, leaving rabbit and potato stashes for the settlers to consume. On one occasion it is claimed they brought a deer carcass for the travelers but as they approached they were shot at, so from that point they opted to keep their distance (Schablitsky, 2012).

This account of being fired upon paints a character of the settlers as being paranoid about the Indigenous people that aligns with Rarick's (2009) telling of the story. From the start of the journey there was concern among the settlers about the violent and untrustworthy Indigenous people that might even try killing settlers if given the chance. Being trapped at Alder Creek, weakened and starving, it is not difficult to imagine settlers feeling extra paranoid about such things. When feeling vulnerable, people become dangerous; it's difficult to imagine feeling more vulnerable than the Donners at Alder Creek that winter. From their oral histories, it is clear that despite not wanting to be seen by the trapped settlers, the *wel mel ti* continued to visit the area regularly to check in on the unfortunate souls while keeping their presence hidden. This practice also ensured they bore witness to the final, most desperate chapters of the party, providing further confirmation that cannibalism did occur Schablitsky, 2012).

Demographic Analysis

Out of grave tragedy can sometimes evolve unique opportunities, this case is no different. The unique opportunity presented by the Donner Party is an anthropological one, more specifically it is possible to conduct demographic analysis and attempt to glean details for how age, gender, and social connections contribute to individual outcomes. It becomes possible to ask uncomfortable questions like which individuals are most likely to survive in such extreme conditions, and who is most likely to perish. The large sample size coupled with the complicated social relationships that existed among party members makes for an interesting case study into the human will to survive.

Grayson (1990) begins with a breakdown of the 87 party members who were trapped in the winter of 1846. It should be noted that due to record keeping practices at the time, the age of some party members is only an estimate as their exact year of birth is unknown. Additionally, the Wolfinger ages are unknown and unaccompanied by estimates. When the age breakdown of the Donner Party is stacked up against census data from the relevant states around the time of the incident, it is found that the population between 11-15 is underrepresented, 21-29 is overrepresented, and 51 and older are underrepresented (Grayson, 1990). The overrepresentation of 20-somethings could be explained as simply a reflection of self-selection for an endeavor such as this. For the most part, families engaging in this journey were seeking to begin a life in California. It is easier to imagine undertaking such a task when you are young and not yet entirely established. Similarly, the single men on the journey all fall within this age category and it is again easy to see why. Rarick (2009) points early in his book to the newspaper advertisement placed by George Donner seeking strong men to drive his wagons and mind his cattle. It sounds like a wonderful adventure, and a great deal. Not only would these men be paid handsomely for their labour on the journey, but they would be getting a free trip to California where the government was offering free land agreements to settlers willing to establish farms. The men who would apply for such work would need to be young, fit, and willing to relocate. The relative lack of teenagers on the journey can also be expected to stem from the self-selection phenomenon of the family groups. There was no shortage of young children in the population, and this coincides with the nature of young non-established families opting to take the trip. No doubt they have children, but their children would tend to be younger. It is also easy to imagine why older populations are relatively underrepresented, again as a matter of self-selection.

Grayson (1990) begins his analysis with three primary assumptions about what can be reasonably expected from such an analysis. There are some assumptions that should be reasonably made when thinking about a scenario such as this, after all we do have a decent understanding of how social structures function, interact, and break down in extreme situations. This type of analysis is useful at the policy level when considering worst case scenarios for natural disasters and other calamities where large populations are involved and isolated with insufficient resources for lengthy periods of time, and can hopefully be used to inform search and rescue efforts to maximize their effectiveness at preserving human lives.

The first assumption Grayson (1990) makes is with regards to age-specific mortality rates. Typically, high death rates are seen in the youngest and oldest populations in a community. General mortality is high between the ages of 1-5 and then begins to decline. Then at age 35 mortality begins to increase consistently as age increases. In stressful situations, these patterns are exaggerated but remain true. This concept is well established in our understanding of mortality as a baseline concept as well as in crisis scenarios, so Grayson (1990) argues we should expect the youngest and oldest members of the Donner Party to experience similar challenges.

The second assumption made relates to sex and mortality. In most populations and across all age demographics, it has been observed that male mortality is significantly higher than female mortality. This is true as a baseline, with females both in the modern and Victorian era on average living longer than males. And again, this pattern is seen to be relevant but exacerbated in emergency situations (Grayson, 1990). So it should be expected that female members of the Donner Party would have a higher rate of survival than the males. Particularly in conditions of nutritional scarcity and extreme cold, both of which should be counted as the greatest stress factors to the Donner Party, women hold biological advantages over men (Grayson, 1990). On the subject of caloric intake, women are smaller than men therefore requiring relatively less food to survive, giving them a clear edge in a famine scenario. If caloric intake is reduced to below recommended levels, but females and males are given the same food resources for an extended period, the males bodies will begin breaking down muscle and fat tissues sooner and at a faster rate than the females. In other words, women in the party can be expected to survive for longer on less food. In addressing the cold, female party members can generally be expected to fare better as well. This is due to higher percentages of subcutaneous fatty tissue among females, offering better natural insulation against the cold. This includes greater concentrations of fatty tissue internally as well, helping protect the major organs. Males in cold conditions have been consistently observed to suffer greater rates of core body temperature decline than females (Grayson, 1990).

There are cultural factors that can contribute to women faring better than men in crisis scenarios as well. Females in western cultures can be expected to express themselves differently and experience different stresses related to their mental health, particularly when a decline in mental health due to scarcity of resources results in violence (Grayson, 1990). Female party members can be expected to resort to violence at far lower rates than male members.

The third assumption Grayson (1990) makes relates to the number of social contacts an individual has, having an inverse impact on their survival. It has been observed in baseline populations in the absence of extreme stressors that the married have a lower mortality rate than the unmarried, and that people with smaller social circles or who are more isolated from friends and family by lifestyle or proximity experience higher mortality than those who have more regular social contact.
As with the other assumptions Grayson makes, the effect of social networking is exaggerated in emergency scenarios. The precise cause of this phenomenon is not fully understood, but it has been theorized that a person who has access to their social network has greater access to information, resources, more timely assistance, and may benefit from a sense of belonging (Grayson, 1990). If the third assumption is true, we should see greater mortality among individuals in smaller family units, those who are unattached as in unmarried or at least having no great attachment to the family unit they were traveling with on the journey, and those who are isolated entirely from all social contact.

Stepping back from statistical analysis for a moment to review a strictly anecdotal scenario from the Donner Party, many of these factors can be observed with regards to the first successful attempt by party members to self-rescue and alert the outside world to the emergency playing out at Truckee Lake. The Forlorn Hope was a group of 17 men, women, and children that attempted to walk out starting on December 16th, 1846. Before leaving, the party constructed 14 pairs of snowshoes for members. Two party members including a ten year old William Murphy turned around and returned to Truckee Lake early on, being without snowshoes proved to be too great an obstacle to their efforts. Before any fatalities occurred, the population of the Forlorn Hope was reduced to 15 (Rarick, 2009).

Of the 15 members who continued on the trail, seven successfully completed the journey and reached safety. Of the fifteen that attempted the journey, ten were male and five were female. The party experienced extreme cold and starvation conditions during the journey, and the gender demographics more than inverted by the end of the endeavor. Of the seven survivors from this group, all five original females survived, but only two of the males (Rarick, 2009). The starvation conditions proved particularly interesting because of the social stress it caused for the party. Two days after their food ran out, Patrick Dolan suggested someone should be sacrificed to feed the rest of the group, another party member suggested a duel to decide who the unlucky party should be. William Eddy suggested the party should simply continue moving and the first to die naturally should be the one consumed. The group agreed nobody should be killed to feed the rest, so no action was taken at that time (Rarick, 2009). Here we see the beginning of the suggestion of violence from a male party member.

Antonio, a 23 year old single male who was hired as an animal handler at the start of the journey was the first to die, with 57 year old Franklin Graves dying soon after. Apparently exhibiting signs of hypothermia, Patrick Dolan became delirious before stripping off his clothes and running off into the woods alone; he did return but died a few hours later. The only child of the party, 12 year old Lemuel Murphy, was close to death. His state created enough social stress to commence the cannibalism, with party members beginning to eat from Dolan's body the night he died (Rarick, 2009).

Fearing for their lives, Salvador and Luis fled the party believing they might be killed and consumed (Rarick, 2009). It was a reasonable assumption on their part, considering Dolan was the first casualty consumed and of the three available bodies at the time he was the only non-white person. Luis and Salvador were Indigenous men who were hired as labourers earlier in the journey and were concerned that their race might make it easier for the majority white party to justify their deaths. Following the departure of Salvador and Luis, William Foster suggested to William Eddy that they should kill three of the remaining women for food. Eddy disagreed with this suggestion, preferring instead the duel approach brought up earlier. He claimed to throw a short club to Foster before advancing on him with a knife to instigate a fight to the death. The women separated the two before any damage was done (Rarick, 2009). Here again we see the male tendency to violent solutions, with the women actively playing a peacemaker role.

25 days after leaving Truckee Lake, the party caught up with Luis and Salvador who were immobile and close to death, not having eaten in more than a week. William Foster shot and killed both men, justifying his action by saying they were as good as dead already and their bodies could be used as a critical food source for the other survivors (Rarick, 2009). It is rare in episodes of survival cannibalism for people to be killed for the purpose of consumption, with the exception being some cases of sailors lost at sea. It is frequently not even necessary to commit murder because by the time starving people are prepared to break the psychological barrier and eat another person there is an ample supply of corpses from which to feed. In the case of the Forlorn Hope, however, the group was under pressure to keep moving and had already begun eating people, so murder was much more easily justified. Other party members did not condone Foster's action, but the six of them did nothing to stop him and there are no reports of anybody refusing to eat of the bodies of Salvador and Luis.

After 33 days of travel, the Forlorn Hope successfully reached civilization and delivered the news that the Donner Party was trapped and starving in the Sierra Nevada. Of the seven survivors, two were male and all five of the females who joined the journey had survived (Rarick, 2009). In fact, the greatest threat to the survival of the women appears to have been the violent cannibalistic desperation exhibited by William Foster, who would conceivably have murdered one or more of the women for food if not for the intervention of the rest of the party. In microcosm we can see the phenomena of Grayson's (1990) assumptions playing out. The oldest and youngest members of the party all died, and women fared far better than men to the degree that at the start of the journey men outnumbered women by two to one, and by the end the women outnumbered the men by nearly three to one.

Having reviewed Grayson's (1990) assumptions, did those assumptions hold up upon analysis of the survivorship demographics of the Donner Party? Let us review the age data first. If this assumption is correct, the youngest and oldest members of the party should experience greater than average mortality. This assumption appears to be correct, with members of the Donner Party in the age category of under five dying at a rate of 62.5% (Grayson, 1990). Also striking is the mortality rate for party members over the age of 49; this group experienced a mortality rate of 100% (Grayson, 1990). This falls neatly in line with the first assumption made by Grayson. While the mortality rate for the youngest members of the party is strikingly high, it also appears to have been better for party members to be very young rather than very old.

As for the age categories in between, there is an interesting spread. The combined average mortality rate for ages 5-9 are 18.2%, 10-14 are 15.4%, 15-19 are 33.3%, 20-29 are 50%, 30-39 are 50%, and 40-49 are 57.1% (Grayson, 1990). The age group with the highest survivability would appear to be teenagers, but there are some interesting departures when the numbers are broken down further.

Here we come upon the second assumption, that women are better suited to survive a cold weather starvation scenario. We have already seen on a smaller scale how members of the Forlorn Hope fared with the cold and starvation. Similar results present themselves when we split the broader picture up along gender lines. The second assumption appears quite sound. Males experienced significantly higher mortality rates than females in all age groups with the exception of age 40-49, where the male fatality rate was 33.3% and the female rate was a staggering 75% (Grayson, 1990). The other exception, of course, is with the older age categories where both men and women died at a rate of 100% (Grayson, 1990).

For the 1-4 age group, males died at a rate of 71.4%, females at 55.6%. Age group 5-9 male mortality was 28.6%, female was 0%. Age group 10-14 male mortality was 25%, compared with 0% for the females. In the age group 15-19 male mortality was 50%, and female was 0%. For 20-29 male mortality was 66.6%, female mortality was just 14.3%. And finally, male mortality for those aged 30-39 was 66.6% and female mortality was 0% (Grayson, 1990). There is a considerable difference between male and female survivability in the Donner party. It is also notable that the timing of deaths looks different along gender lines as well. Men began dying much earlier than the women, which is perhaps a reflection of women being better suited to these specific conditions. The men clearly not only begin to starve to death sooner, but based on the available data they decline much faster as well. From December 1846 until January 1847, 14 men died and no women. Then from February to March 1847 11 men died and 10 women (Grayson, 1990). Grayson (1990) also notes that cultural factors can be observed in the mortality of men versus women in the period leading up to the winter entrapment. Of the five men who had died already on the journey, four were directly or indirectly caused by violence. This number accounts for 13.3% of the total male deaths in the Donner Party. If we add the murder of Salvador and Luis to the pot of party members who died by violence, the number balloons to 18.8% of all male deaths among the Donner Party, making male aggression a significant risk factor for male party members (Grayson, 1990).

The mortality rate among males between the ages of 20 and 39 are unexpectedly high, and not just when compared with the females in the same age categories. This is where the third assumption can be brought into the equation. Alongside simple age and gender factors, the social element can be seen to contribute to the high mortality rate of the middle group of males. Among the party members, males in this age group were disproportionately unmarried hired hands with no other connection to the Donner Party aside from their employment relationship (Grayson, 1990). This means there was not as strong a social structure built up around these individuals, they were not being checked on and communicated with as regularly, they would not have felt as strong a sense of belonging as party members who were traveling with family. The third assumption appears to neatly answer the question of why strong and relatively healthy males in their prime suffered such catastrophic mortality rates on the expedition.

In conclusion, the mortality of members of the Donner Party, and by extension any community facing an extreme cold starvation scenario, was most immediately affected by gender, age, and scale of social connection (Grayson, 1990). Clear patterns of mortality can be observed when broken down into these three assumptions, where otherwise the information may appear chaotic. The interplay between these three factors has a significant impact on the survivability of emergency scenarios including exposure to the elements and scarcity of food resources. Grayson (1990) presents an elegant, considered explanation for what factors impacted the members of the Donner Party most significantly.

Conclusion

The Donner Party has earned a place in the history books as one of the most tragic stories of the colonization of North America. As a contemporary event, it became a touchstone for the promotion of American mythology and values, and a driver of accelerating Manifest Destiny including the reimagined character of America and accompanying Christian nationalism contained therein. Victims of the journey were subjected to the impossible human calculus of life and death decisions, who should be saved, who should be abandoned, what responsibility did they have to one another, and how to give themselves and their families the best chance of survival.

Facing months of starvation and freezing temperatures, many were forced to cannibalize their fallen family members and friends. The exact prevalence of cannibalism has proven difficult to prove due to a variety of factors, including acidity of the soil and the extreme degree of processing that went into pulling every possible calorie out of potential food sources. Despite the scientific challenges in proving cannibalism occurred by modern scientific standards, there was nobody involved in the actual events that disputed the fact that cannibalism occurred, although there were some that denied personally having participated. At the same time, the media was more than happy to sensationalize the story, further muddying the waters of how much cannibalism did take place.

Demographic analysis of looking into who lived and who died offers some interesting insights into who is best positioned to succeed in an extreme cold starvation scenario. Baseline data tells us the very old and very young experience higher mortality rates than the rest of the population, and that men are subject to both biological and social pressures that lower their survivability. The extreme nature of this scenario distorts the mortality rates of all demographics, but baseline conclusions around gender, age, and social connections prove to hold true. Those best suited to survive in this scenario proved to be women, in the middle age groups of teenagers, 20's, and 30's, and with stronger social connections. Those more likely to die after the youngest and oldest party members were men, who had a high mortality rate even in the middle age groups, who had no strong family connections present in the community.

The events of the Donner Party are a reminder of the importance of planning, social connection, and discipline. It is also an interesting opportunity to study the myths of American expansionism during the 19th century, and consider the consequences of that expansion. Many myths of the American character originating in Manifest Destiny echo forward into the modern imagination of what it means to be an American.

References:

Dixon, K. J., Novak, S. A., Robbins, G., Schablitsky, J. M., Scott, G. R., & Tasa, G. L. (2010). "Men, Women, and Children Starving": Archaeology of the Donner Family Camp. *American Antiquity*, 75(3), 627–656. https://doi.org/10.7183/0002-7316.75.3.627

Ellis, M.A.B., Merritt, C.W., Novak S.A., & Dixon, K.J. (2011). The Signature of Starvation: A Comparison of Bone Processing at a Chinese Encampment in Montana and the Donner Party Camp in California. *Historical Archaeology*, 45(2), 97–112.

Grayson, D. (1990). Donner Party Deaths: A Demographic Assessment. *Journal of Anthropological Research*, 46(3), 223–242.

Kelly, A. B. (2006). Cannibalism in the Sierra Nevadas: The Donner Party. *Forensic Examiner*, 15(3), 63–65.

King, J. & Steed, J. (1995). John Baptiste Trudeau of the Donner Party: Rascal or Hero? *California History*, 74(2), 162–173. https://doi.org/10.2307/25177490

Rarick, E. (2009). *Desperate passage: The Donner Party's perilous journey West*. Oxford: Oxford University Press.

Schablitsky, J. M. (2012). A new look at the Donner Party. *Archaeology*, 65(3), 54.

Stuckey, M. E. (2011). The Donner Party and the Rhetoric of Westward Expansion. *Rhetoric & Public Affairs*, 14(2), 229–260. https://doi.org/10.1353/rap.2010.0224

Voeller, C.R. (2009). "A man is a fool who prefers poor California beef to human flesh": (Re) Definitions of Masculinity in Nineteenth-Century US Donner Party Literature. *Western American Literature*, 44(3), 200–223.

Wilsey, J. D. (2017). "Our Country Is Destined to be the Great Nation of Futurity": John L. O'Sullivan's Manifest Destiny and Christian Nationalism, 1837-1846. Religions, 8(4), 68. https://doi.org/10.3390/rel8040068